Mine

Jane McKie

Published by Cinnamon Press
www.cinnamonpress.com

ISBN 978-1-78864-171-5

British Library Cataloguing in Publication Data. A CIP record for this book can be obtained from the British Library.

Designed and typeset in Bodoni by Cinnamon Press. Cover design by Adam Craig.

Cinnamon Press is represented by Inpress Ltd.

Acknowledgements

Warm thanks to Jan Fortune and the Cinnamon family, and a huge shout out to all my writing friends—in solidarity, and with abiding love.

About the Author

Jane McKie has written several poetry collections, including *Morocco Rococo* (2007), *Kitsune* (2015), and *Quiet Woman, Stay* (2020) with Cinnamon. Her most recent full collection is *Carnation Lily Lily Rose* (Blue Diode, 2023). She lives in Scotland, but was originally from the Sussex coast, which inspired a number of the poems here.

Contents

*I discovered many wonders at the seaside,
not least my beautiful Shell.*

Mine

Immaculate

When we left, before we'd turned in the keys,
I went through the rooms with a bucket and bleach,

treating the moth-print mania of neglected walls.
Some mildew climbed to the ceiling

and I had to lever a cloth on a broom.
I wondered, then, about leaving things clean,

about the perfect erasure we all expect —
things handed on as if they're pristine,

as if a whole family hasn't kissed or breathed
or cried or vented within the walls,

and before us, another family, even more messy,
their stories ascending to rooftops, further —

into the sky where no broom can reach.

Keys on the counter, boxes unboxing

You are spinning in the middle of the hallway, in your cocoon —
chrysalis of longing, spectral chime. This time we'll settle, call it
home. The carpets go on forever without stands of wooden legs
in place. We ask if you'll lend a hand. Instead you turn your face
to the naked lightbulb and shrug your wings. Later, after unpacking,
we feast on takeaway pizza; unspun and hungry, you climb down.

Mine

On nights when the wind drops, I hear it crooning softly,
not like a real bomb. A toothless, barnacled silhouette, wittering
to itself when the tide is low. My friends and I sometimes get close,
daring each other to nudge its rust. But what happens when
the music cuts out? Tonight, the mine's a mute companion:
whiff of brine, cryptic fist. As my eyelids close, that's when it—

Over and over, like a mighty sea

An arch to our church door
like an upturned jaw

      or a ninth wave

before it breaks.

Inside: the distant trill
of crickets; summer heat.

Even a mile from the sea,
the warm nave's shadows

taste of salt.
Cut flowers wilt.

There is no such thing
as refuge or retreat.

The season

In the first beach hut

Door ajar, lying in sunlight: a lean Setter, its flayed-red
ribcage heaving.

In the second beach hut

The fat paper bolus of a wasp's nest. Bullets squeeze
through a tiny wound in its side, buzzing.

In the third beach hut

Only the breeze — dejected — picking up dust, picking up
newsprint. Setting them both down again unread.

Waves of sand and snow

After Vaughan Cornish's Waves of Sand and Snow (1914)

This is where wind presses its cheek to the sand.
Where sand attempts to form a spine.

It's good for thinking
and for not thinking.

~

When running towards the incoming tide, what rushes
a body is met by the chest, rises up

to dissolve the word
'breath'.

~

So many blessings here: lungful of clean air;
single white sail, far out, cresting a pale green

band of sea; ridges underfoot that greet
small bones and pummel them in harmony.

A place to bring loneliness and release it
into the greater loneliness of constant movement.

~

In summer, the strand is claimed
by brightly coloured towels

like flags from a republic of workers
who come to break their graft

upon margins. Their children gallop,
dropping petals of poppy-red ice.

~

In winter, the shore is a silver blister.
Bunched dunes and marram mimic
a white-veined congress of roses.

Frozen, sand tries being snow for a day.
It's like trying on a pale, sequined coat
only to find it prickly, uncomfortable.

~

The beach receives cuts with infinite grace,
its patterns bisected by fishermen's spades:

in with the sharp edge, out with the worms.
The tender sand will always close.

Kelp heart

What is not a muscle and is not a rubber
flag and is not a coiled, gutted snake
and is not a ball of phlegm. What is not
trivial. What does not succumb to stones,
but allows a stone to be an anchor. What,
if it does succumb to stones, wears holes
easily, as if they can be filled. What tries
to grow into all the colours, especially those
of autumn and weeping. What resembles
a flame underwater and is tireless in love.

Polished malachite

on my desk, riven
with almost-blue, a pool
or algal cistern.

I touch it when I'm sad
and its green eye blinks, rippling
with souterrain light.

Starlings in flight

Like the flinch of a dreaming
eyelid, two harpooned
whales of iron filings

scatter. Moving towards you,
their pattern shifts again, reforms.
And when the busy loom

throws its cloth across
your head, you're netted
in such sound and shadow

it's as if a god's mouth
passes close to your ear
and breathes your name.

From the other side

After Spiritual paintings by Georgiana Houghton

If you could speak, it would be as cornucopia,
kaleidoscope, mechanical wave.

All the ways of speaking would be yours: all the colours, all the shapes.

If you could speak, it would be a swallow's breath, the movement
of a hand across a page, a flower among sedges caught in a sluice.

I walk into my office, and there you are, talking in corners.

I walk home, and there you are, reciting every route.

Thysania Agrippina (white witch moth)

The man grieving for his mother
sees her face everywhere.
Today, she flutters at his elbow,
transforming his office into
a humid, thrumming habitat:
monkey's screech; press of trees.

When the purple light she carries
flickers through the canopy,
the man weeps until leaves
begin to fall, and the forest slowly fades;
until all that's left is a cluttered desk
and a cursor pulsing on the page.

Godzilla vs Mothra

Suffer small bluish,
its fruitless death.

You bring me reds
hoping I'll smile,

coppers to the plate,
wing-stuck, vibrating

on this stormy moth day,
this pity-party in which

insects are weak
and you are strong,

little Toho monster,
anti-Mothra, slayer

of garden Lepidoptera.
I take your fat palms —

pink, sloppy-hearted
peonies — and extract

the last crushed
cabbage white —

its leaves and cinders —
loving you

even as I tell you,
stop.

Kevlar

I am the tattoo of a spider's web
on a sixteen-year-old girl's calf.
Traced from a drawing of a photo,
in time, I will thread up her thigh,
over her whole torso, in a riot of
silk that is stronger than Kevlar.

She will wear me like armour:
my vest of ink, her toughest skin.
Who wouldn't fear a woman
fluent in the language of spiders?
Those twitches in cobwebs
that throb like old wounds.

Butterfly

The doubled daughter
caught in a lens in a mirror
has the sun behind her.
She's lost her features
to shadow, but the dress
is a proxy for the girl:
cloudscape seen from
a plane, as substantial
as mountains; a frozen
kinetic field in which
the photographic body
is missing. Massing
on my shelves, in my
hard drive: beloved, ink-
pressed doppelgängers.

Wildfire

This orange city —
particulates blotting
skyscrapers —
has never looked
so mellow:
steel giants
are warm shadows;
the waterfront,
a bleeding line
of violet.
Atoms hive into
depots of smoke,
until, to the woman
at a window
she's advised not
to open, fire —
just for a moment —
is pure abstraction.

Fool's spring

The hawthorn is athwart with cream, its petals, tiny pink
and white panes through which sun breathes, palely.
How easy it is to misread warmth, to fold away woollens
along with old hurts. The hawthorn wants only the buds,
never the ice, and, like a child, opens up to early light.

Dreaming in an age of austerity

Not a single one finished: all mark time
until a rich developer completes the job.
Here, stone knuckles. There, exposed metal rods
stab at the sky like a mech-monster's fingers.

Not vital or hungry, these resort Titans.
But not quite dead either. Gulls like to roost
in the pockets of them. Gulls dabble bills in
puddles that form from the absence of roofs.

Even small children play in the undead bodies
of imagined buildings, sneaking past tape
to be mummies and daddies in beautiful houses
that shelter insatiable, suckling doll-babies.

Back in the day, we never drank in Jamaica Bar

but before it closed down it held sweat, held thighs tight
to red vinyl cushions. Before it closed down, it was the spot,
the place, the corner-joint loved by every kind of visitor:
men resolving into boys, women leaning head-to-head
in its small agora. Their voices would sift and ebb, mark
the time. Clothed only in the pastels of each other's lives,
they were the sun-lovers who kept our island afloat —
revellers, lotus-eaters, they opened, lotus-like, on the bar's
damp benches. Now they're gone, the place is a crone,
a plastered-over billboard of itself. So — please come,
pass through, walk under its roof crossing yourselves
as you encounter the pale red ghost of impossible wine.

Let me tell you about the weather where we are

It's the slow beginning of a dance, the part where the couple
come together, placing hand into hand, hand onto hip,

drawing separate bodies close, their colours characteristically
lush for this part of the world, as if romance is hardwired.

When the overture gives way to something compelling,
taste buds wake up; saliva flows. And then the dip:

an arched back — bowed so low, sky and earth are almost
conjoined. Thunder. Brief downpour. Silence.

After this pause, the pace quickens again and brings the pair
into orbit, twirling auras like skirts of water, skeins of heat.

You can't make the two out: faces, one face; bodies, one body.
This is what it's like to live here. This flashpoint, our sunrise.